Beginner Samplers

Young girls were much more apt to be schooled in the use of a needle in days past than they are today. The everyday need for sewing is a passing memory in today's "ready to wear" world.

Back then, catalogs offered an array of starter samplers or kits designed to get girls sewing. They included scissors, tiny thimbles, needles, floss assortments and projects to attempt. Often these came arranged in small tins or cardboard carriers embossed with wonderful and very colorful graphics.

These kits are darling and are a favorite of collectors today. The projects included samplers, doll clothes, doll linens, or small blocks stamped with a variety of delightful subjects designed to keep a child interested.

Whether the results ended up on a doll, framed, or joined together in a quilt, they were an accomplishment to be proud of. What a way to learn your stitches!

Puppy Love

This little guy looks smitten. We can only guess which lovely little lass has his eyes lit up!
pattern on page 23

Forest Fawn

This little "deer" is up and about. She's met her match in the butterflies.
pattern on page 22

Dancing Duck & Puppy

What better way to lead a parade than with a candy baton. This darling pup is ready to prance, go to a dance or just walk on a leash to and fro!
patterns on pages 20 - 21

Plump Pillows

Pillows were and still are a popular way to decorate a home. They are inexpensive and can be done up in endless ways to fit any room or decorating style. Because they are so useful, they have always been a focus for needleworkers. Numerous articles in women's magazines dealt with designs for and advice on pillows. For instance: "It has been said, 'Adaptability is the keynote of success.' Certainly, the woman with a big accumulation of different pillows varying in size, design, and texture has struck the keynote of successful comfort for her family, and her guests. Any cushion may contain in its interior makeup all the essentials for the comfort of the tired head or back, yet it should also be pretty. Every pillow should be an artistic creation, not a make-shift, no matter how inexpensive are the materials from which it is evolved. Save some pillows for everyday use and do not bedeck the covers with costly embroidery. Keep your show pillows for the parlor."

The Modern Priscilla June 1907
While this advice may seem a bit stern, it does make its point! It also shows that the role of the pillow and its decoration hasn't changed much in the last hundred years.

Kitty and Kittens

This cat is a perfect fit with its gingham pillow.
Snuggled together on a hammock is a great way to while away a lazy summer afternoon. Tinting adds depth to the design so you can almost feel the breeze.
patterns on pages 24 - 28

Kitty Romance

"Why sir, you do make me blush!" Animal romance and weddings were very popular for towel motifs and seemed to hit their peak in the 1940s.
pattern on page 26

Cats in a Basket

What a delightful pairing. Anyone who has ever had cats knows how much they love to play in baskets.

pattern on page 30

Cat with Bow

This guy is certainly interested in something. What makes this pillow stand out is the border design. Borders or trim can completely change the look of a pillow. They add so much and are worth the extra effort.

pattern on page 29

Cat on a Ruffled Pillow

Ruffles add a beautiful finish to this pillow. They competed with lace as the most popular trim from the 1920s and 1930s.

pattern on page 31

Plush Pillows

The fascination with humanizing pets became popular in the 1920s. These plump and plush pillows show pups doing what we do: playing, relaxing, and chores.

These active animals were not limited to juvenile items, but showed up throughout the house, especially in the kitchen. (This may have been wishful thinking for ladies looking for a hand with chores!) Needlework or "fancywork" catalogs contained an array of potholders, towels, toaster covers, etc. sporting all manner of animals doing all the daily chores that homemakers did.

Musical and Relaxing Pups

These talented "K-9" musicians are swinging. This pillow would look great in a family room or a boy's room.

Mr. Bowser is sitting back in his favorite chair at the end of the day with his pipe and his paper - truly the king of his castle. I wonder who fetches a dog's slippers?

patterns on pages 32-33

Dogs and Butterflies

What a trooper! Between the butterflies darting and the the babe messing, it's hard to keep your mind on your sewing. Good Luck.

pattern on pages 34 - 35

Cowboy

Cowboy puppies and kittens were surprisingly popular. Maybe it's that urge we all have to rope and ride. The romance of the cowboy seems to have been a bigger draw in days gone by when the open range was not as distant a place as it is now.

pattern on page 35

Pups in a Basket

This design combines two favorite motifs in needlework: animals and baskets. This style of puppy with the large expressive eyes became popular with designers in the 1940s. It's hard to resist a gift in a basket, especially when it's grinning like these two. These pillows were used to decorate bedrooms.

pattern on page 36

Pups with Heart

This style comes to us from the 1950s. The pudgy faces and bodies from the 1940s began to change. The bodies stretch out and lose their stodgy proportions. Thin or thick, they're hard to resist. The combination of pups and patchwork make a great "retro" feeling.

pattern on page 37

Baby Quilts

Baby quilts were and still are a great favorite. They serve a dual purpose: they add color and style to the nursery, and both teach and entertain children. Animals were a favorite and natural subject for nursery decor. Victorian redwork "penny squares" showed very realistic renderings of domestic and exotic creatures. This realism gave way to the very stylized "deco" designs of the 1920s, and by the 1930s and 1940s, the animals became characters in and of themselves.

They often showed up in clothes and were working or playing just like real people. In the late 1940s and 1950s the pudge gives way a bit and, like many modern styles, details are fewer. While thinner and a little sparser, these animals lose none of their charm.

Baby quilts as a gift are truly treasured. What better way to welcome a wee one than to greet them with your own creation. As a gift for someone else's child or an heirloom for your own, quilts are a perfect baby gift. They are a tradition that is ageless and appear in many catalogs and mail order brochures. Both transfers and complete kits were offered. Bucilla and Herrschner catalogs, in particular, seemed to pride themselves on their children's items.

Beginning in the 1920s and continuing through the 1940s, their selection of tinted baby quilts and crib sheets are wonderful. The quilts displayed on these pages show a great range of styles. They stitch up beautifully with simple stem stitches and a few French knots.

Any of these designs would also lend itself to tinting with crayons. Give it a try and create something that children will want to keep hold of and pass on to future generations.

Take a look at all the babies
Trying to catch your eye,
Between their charm and sassy looks
They sure give it a try.
So grab your needle, thread it quick
And start your stitching now,
Get these little critters done,
Before they have a cow!

Baby Animals Quilt

This quilt gets your attention with just a few colors and stitches. Pick your favorite color and make sure you choose fabric with a pattern for the alternate blocks. These designs complement the colorful and dense designs popular in the 1920s and 1930s. There is a great array of reproduction fabrics available to quilters now that are aimed at juvenile quilts, something for almost anyone's taste. Aunt Grace's and Moda lines of fabric are a great place to start looking for that perfect cotton.

patterns on pages 38 - 43

Cute Animals Quilt

Simple stem stitches and a few colors are all it takes to produce a lovely, interesting baby cover. These animals would keep any child happy as well as cozy. If you use a dense pattern or a solid color for the sashing, you will be happier if you pick brightly colored floss for the embroidery. This will make the blocks stand out beautifully and really catch the eye.

patterns on pages 44 - 55

Cute little boy and girl bears work and play in each block of this charming quilt.

Stitch them in soft colors for a sweet baby girl or in brighter colors for a playful baby boy.

patterns on pages 56 - 62

Baby Bears

These cubbies have a busy day,
They work a bit but mostly play.

By nighty night they're pretty beat
They nod their heads and drag their feet.

They grab their candle, say their prayers
And head for bed atop the stairs.

Oh, to be a teddy bear!

Busy Kitties

The busy little kittens all over this quilt are certainly putting in a day's work.

No wonder they need a good quilt to put them to bed. The use of elaborate quilting in the alternate blocks of this quilt is a lovely complement to the embroidery.

patterns on pages 68 - 71

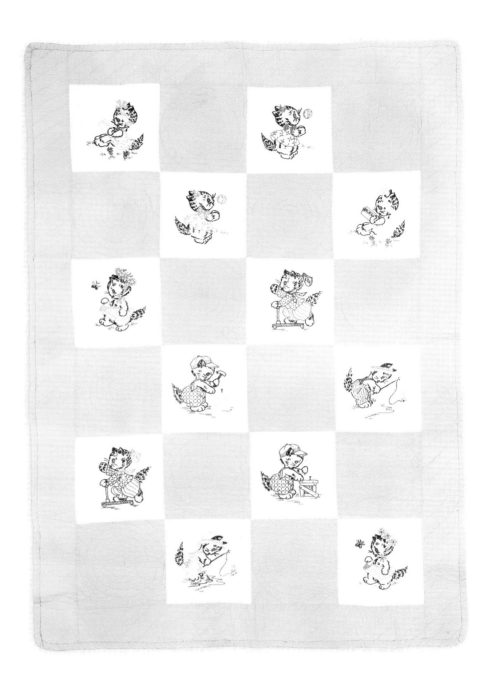

Numbers Summer Topper

This lightweight cutie is perfect for summertime. This little "number" will not only keep a child comfy but give him a step up on his math.

patterns on pages 63 - 67

The Little Town

Do you know a little town
Called, they tell me, Snuggledown?
It's where the sandman lives, they say
And children go at close of day.

How to get there? Simple, quite!
Shut your sleepy eyes up tight,
Tucked in bed in your nightgown,
There you are in Snuggledown!

Constance Vivien Frazier
Needlecraft August 1930

Dog with Butterflies

Bags aren't just bags anymore. This one is much too precious for dirty socks. Combining a vintage reproduction fabric with this cute dog will work just as well for a wall hanging or a tote!

pattern on page 73

Dogs and Cats

Decorative bags work for a variety of uses besides laundry: toys, blankets, quilts, etc. They look great just hanging from a hook!

These designs are typical of the styles found in the late 1930s and early 1940s. The red and black colors were immensely popular when depicting scotties. After Roosevelt's dog, Fala, hit the papers, scotties were all the rage in decoration. They could be found on linens, quilts, towels, calendars, cards - just about anything!

patterns on pages 74 - 75

Kitty Face and Two Pups Hanging Laundry Bags

This kitty is a way to give stuffed animals a purpose. It's a "purrfect" mix, don't you think?

Bags like this one and on the opposite page were meant to be put on hangers in the closet. What a great idea - out of sight!

patterns on pages 76 - 79

Laundry Bags

What can you say about laundry bags other than you don't see them much anymore. I'm not sure why their popularity has faded, but I believe it's because of both the amount of and the ease with which laundry is done today.

Before modern washers and dryers, people had fewer clothes and made those last a bit longer. Tell that to the teenagers of today.

They could never fit a week's worth of laundry in one of these bags! But in the first four decades of this century, these bags were extremely popular and came in an infinite variety of shapes and decorations.

The most charming, of course, are the children's bags.

This sampling of pet motifs is a great collection to choose from and will take you right back to those days when combining pets and laundry still made sense!

Little Faces Potholders

This kitty is red-faced. I wonder what she's been up to! Or maybe she's just reminding us with her big eyes to watch out what we're handling. Either way she is irresistible.

Potholders are a quick and thoughtful gift to make for your favorite friends. People love to get gifts that are handmade. It makes them feel special. Stitching these up takes a little fabric, a bit of floss and not much time. Get going!

patterns on pages 80 - 81

Bears at Play

Crib quilts often have a border made of a coordinating fabric. This one combines a border with a stitched frame, creating a "portrait" effect that's very fetching.

pattern on pages 82 - 83

Three Little Pigs

Clever animal tales were a common theme for crib sheets. The design on this topper are a perfect place to use crayon tinting. The effect is wonderful.

pattern on pages 84 - 85

Baby Play

Sewing for the baby,
All the livelong day —
Such a pleasant labor
That it's only play.

Pretty things for baby,
For carriage, crib and chair —
Dainty things, to cover him,
Pretty things to wear.

Clever decoration
In simple stitchery —
Why wouldn't baby's sewing
Be only play for me?

Summer Quilts

This poetic sentiment seems appropriate when talking about Summer Quilts or "crib sheets", as they were labeled in catalogs of days gone by. They were a favorite for needleworkers - they were fun to stitch and fast to finish, because no batting or quilting was required.

Quilts were often sold in kits with vibrant decorations pre-stamped on a light colored background fabric of unbleached muslin or batiste.

The samples included here are animals; however, nursery rhymes, ABCs, Numbers, Fairy Tales, and cartoon/movie characters were also found on the pages of women's catalogs and magazines.

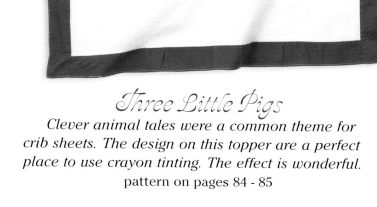

Bunnies on a Bicycle

Add a double rickrack border to add color.

pattern on pages 86 - 87

Seesaw

Add color with an embroidered border.

pattern on pages 88 - 89

Potholders

Potholders have been and always will be a necessity in every kitchen, old or new. They are also seen as a decorative accent. The sets which include pads and holders are a vintage favorite. The sets contained two or three pads and a sleeve or board with hooks.

Combinations were endless and often used both tinting and embroidery; they were sold more often than not as a kit. They are an easy way to add a bit of retro kitsch to your kitchen.

Scotties

Said one dog to the other
Welcome to my home.
Stop and visit, stay a while,
We're happy you could come.

We love to have you as a guest
Your visits we await.
Our only hope is when you leave
You stop and latch the gate!

Potholders

patterns on pages 90 - 91

Sampler Blocks for Quilts

It's unfortunate that young girls are no longer schooled in the art of needlework as a matter of course. Before our age of relatively cheap and abundant clothing, linens, pillow, etc., sewing was a necessity for the keeping of a home.

Misses were started early with a needle, and a deft hand was both admired and coveted. It also reflected on the mother!

One way to learn was using small projects or "samplers" to teach techniques that were relatively easy and in small enough portions that a child's attention span was not overly taxed.

The traditional sampler used for this purpose fell out of favor in the early part of the 20th century and small blocks with illustrations replaced them. These blocks were perfect for doll or nursery quilts and snuck the arts of sewing and quilting into the mix.

Fun Friends Sampler Blocks

Animals were and still are the favorite theme for children's crafts.

The blocks pictured above would be a charming way to pass along the art of embroidery to someone - or catch up on your own skills!

They make great little throws or pillows.

patterns on pages 92 - 93

Dog and Cat
Listening to the Radio

This radio vignette would be a lovely addition to the den of your favorite dog or cat lover - preferably one with teenagers!

pattern on page 95

Puppy Bib

Does your toddler like dogs? Encourage him to keep the bib on with this cute doggie design.

pattern on pages 94 - 95

Kitten and Scotty Dog

photo on page 2

Kitten and Scotty

Only on a pillow will these two sit so amiably!

Dogs and cats were by far the most popular animals for needlework, especially with children.

pattern is full size

Dancing Duck

photo on page 3

pattern is full size

Take a stitch and pull it out
Will this never end?
Learning seems such a trial
It makes my needle bend.

Will I ever sew a seam
As well as mother dear?
Sometimes I truly think
The time is nowhere near!

🍪 **TRIMMING** 🍪

The fabric of my life
    is grey —
Hard work in one
    small place.
I'll concentrate on
    trimming it
With lots of laughs
    for lace.

pattern is full size

'Tinting with Crayons

Crayons Aren't Paints - Even though ironing softens the crayon, their hard nature means that some of the texture of the fabric and the strokes you make will show through - just like when you make a rubbing over a penny. Making your strokes in the same direction can be challenging in large areas, which is why projects with smaller individual areas of color are best suited to crayon tinting.

Tip: Practice on extra muslin first.

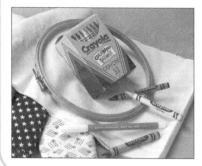

Supplies - Muslin fabric, 24 colors of crayons (or more), embroidery floss, embroidery hoop, micron pen, needle

Crayon Hints - Besides being convenient, crayons come in beautiful colors and aren't intimidating. Simply color in the spaces to create the look you want.

pattern is full size

Build Up Color, Edges In

Add layers of crayon color with the strokes going in one direction, or opposite directions for a darker effect. Start lightly - you can always add more. Shading built up from the edges inward helps model or add depth to pieces, so that the tinted areas are not only colorful but three-dimensional as well. You can even choose to leave an area completely open to give a strong highlight.

Use the Correct End

For filling in color, the blunt end of the crayon works best and it works even better if its hard edge is rounded off a little before you start. Keep the pointed end for details or adding a fine shaded line to edges.

Tip: Let the Fabric Do the Work

A shaded fabric (white on white or off white) adds depth to your shading. Larger designs are a little better than fine ones because they give more variety.

1. Position fabric over a pattern, secure corners with masking tape.

Trace pattern outline directly onto muslin with a blue-line water erase pen or a pencil.

2. Place fabric on a pad of extra fabric and color areas with regular children's crayons.

Color the pattern well with crayon color.

3. Sandwich the fabric between two sheets of plain paper.

Iron on 'cotton' setting to 'set' the crayon colors.

4. If desired, back design with another piece of fabric, place fabric or layers in an embroidery hoop.

Use 3-ply floss to outline the design.

pattern is full size

Sassy Kitty
photo on page 4

pattern is full size

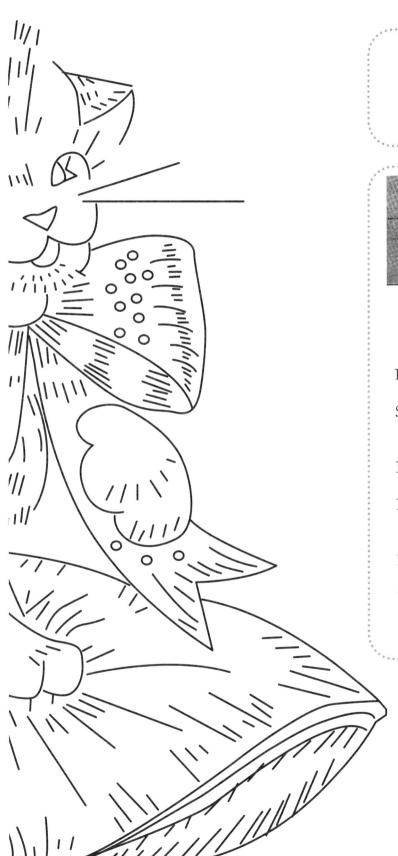

Sassy Kitty

photo on page 4

*This sassy cat on her throne
Invites you to sit down.
Pull up a chair and rest your head,
Just watch out for that crown!*

How Kitty Thinks

BY ANNA L. CURTIS

I like to watch my kitty think.
   Her tail goes to and fro;
Sometimes it switches like a whip,
   Sometimes it's very slow.

It's slow when she just thinks like this—
   "Now, what shall I do next?"
It's faster when she begs for food,
   And fastest when she's vexed.

Even a dream will stir her tail;
   The tip sways daintily.
I'm sure a cat thinks with her tail.
   Just watch *your* cat and see.

Kitty Romance

photo on page 4

Needlecraft Embroidery Book

Kitchen Sampler 20c

No. C410. Who can resist this yellow pussy against a red and blue fireplace and rug with yellow percale top for stool. Stamped on unbleached muslin 12-by-14 inches with percale patches for applique, **20 cents.** Floss, 15¢.

pattern is full size

Care of Linens

Washing

• Test for colorfastness on the seam allowance. Let several drops of water fall through the fabric onto white blotter paper. If color appears, the fabric is not colorfast.

• To set dye, soak fabric in water and vinegar.

• Wash with a very mild detergent or soap, using tepid water. Follow all label instructions carefully.

• Do not use chlorine bleach on fine linen. Whiten it by hanging it in full sunlight.

Stain Removal

• Grease - Use a presoak fabric treatment and wash in cold water.

• Non-greasy - Soak in cold water to neutralize the stain. Apply a presoak and then wash in cold water.

• Ballpoint Ink - Place on an absorbent material and soak with denatured or rubbing alcohol. Apply room temperature glycerin and flush with water. Finally, apply ammonia and quickly flush with water.

• Candle Wax - Place fabric between layers of absorbent paper and iron on low setting. Change paper as it absorbs wax. If a stain remains, wash with peroxide bleach.

• Rust - Remove with lemon juice, oxalic acid or hydrofluoric acid.

Storage

• Wash and rinse thoroughly in soft water.

• Do not size or starch.

• Place cleaned linen on acid-free tissue paper and roll loosely.

• Line storage boxes with a layer of acid-free tissue paper.

• Place rolled linens in a box. Do not stack. Weight causes creases.

• Do not store linens in plastic bags.

• Hang linen clothing in a muslin bag or cover with a cotton sheet.

Woman's World July 1932

Two Kittens on a Hammock

photo on page 4

enlarge pattern to 160%

enlarge pattern to 160%

Cats in a Basket

photo on page 5

A cat in a basket
Who ever heard of that
Next thing you know
They'll wear bows and hats!

enlarge pattern to 160%

enlarge pattern
to 160%

Musical Pups

photo on page 6

Toot your horn,
Tickle those keys.
Dogs making music
Is a sight to see.

Sit back, relax and light your pipe
It's been a busy day,
Your paper's here and dinner's on
The kids are home from play.

The end of day is welcome,
Mister needs a break;
Before you eat, rest a while
And your pleasure take!

enlarge pattern to 160%

Children's Page

By Elizabeth
C. Wherry

Time for Daddy

I T'S time for Daddy,
It's time for Daddy,
Let's run to the window
and see.
We'll watch for Daddy
We'll listen for Daddy
My big brown doggie
and me.

My ears try hard
To hear my Daddy
But they lie still and flat.
My dog lifts one ear
Up for Daddy—
But mine won't lift like that.

Family Weekly November 1934

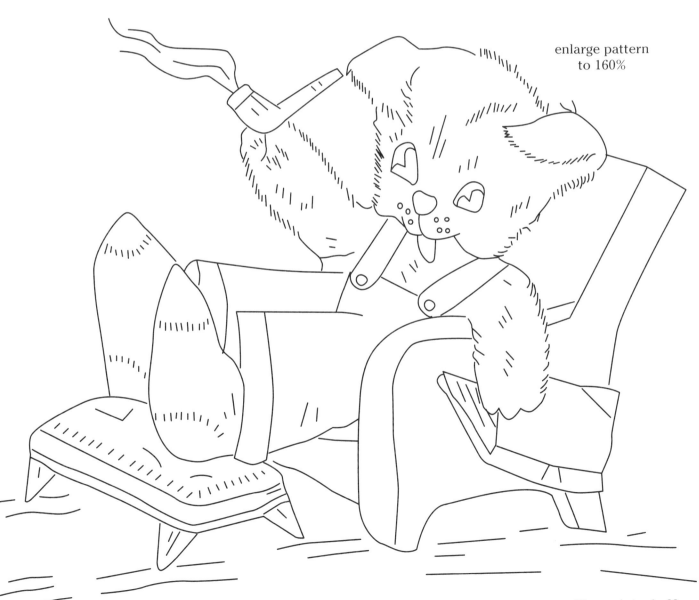

enlarge pattern
to 160%

Dogs and Butterflies
photo on page 6

position
butterfly
as shown
in photo

pattern is full size

enlarge pattern to 160%

Pups in a Basket
photo on page 7

enlarge pattern to 160%

enlarge pattern to 160%

"One doesn't need to be a skilled embroideress to achieve success in the very ancient and very fashionable art of quilting - the prize invariably goes to the good plain sewer who can run rows and rows and rows of tiny even stitches all in perfect apple pie order." Modern Priscilla August 1928

Baby Animals Quilt

photo on page 8

FINISHED SIZE: 34" x 54"

FABRICS:
1 yard White for embroidered blocks
⅔ yard Light Blue print for alternating blocks and borders
Yellow for backing and binding:
1⅛ yards 60" wide OR 2 yards 45" wide

MATERIALS:
Embroidery floss
Embroidery needle
35" x 55" Batting

CUTTING:
Embroidered blocks:
10 White squares 8¾" x 11"
Print blocks:
10 squares 8" x 10½"
Print borders:
Top/bottom strips 2½" x 30½"
2 side strips 2½" x 54½"
Yellow backing and batting:
Pieced to fit 35" x 55"
Binding:
Yellow 2½" strips sewn together to make 180" (5 yards)

INSTRUCTIONS:
1. Trace the pattern onto each White block. Embroider. Press.
   Trim blocks to 8" x 10½".
2. Sew 4 blocks together to make each row. See Row Assembly diagram.
3. Sew the rows together following the Quilt Assembly diagram.
4. Sew the top and bottom borders to the quilt. Press.
5. Sew the side borders to the quilt. Press.
6. Layer backing, batting and top to form a sandwich.
   Baste the layers together. Quilt as desired.
   Trim the backing and batting to the edge of the quilt top.
7. Sew binding strips into one 180" long piece.
   Press binding in half lengthwise.
   Sew binding to the quilt front.
   Turn to the back and sew in place.

Row Assembly Diagram

E + P + E + P
P + E + P + E
E + P + E + P
P + E + P + E
E + P + E + P

E = Embroidered Block
P = Print Fabric Block

Quilt Assembly Diagram

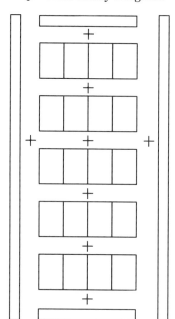

pattern is full size

pattern is full size

pattern is full size

Baby Animals Quilt
photo on page 8

The Sweetest Place
A meadow for the little lambs,
A honey hive for bees,
And pretty nests for singing birds
Among the leafy trees.
There's rest for all the little ones
In one place or another,
But who has half so sweet a place
As baby with her mother!

WAITING
BY NANCY BARNHART

*Mistress, while you sip
your tea,
Many tales relating,
Do you never think of me,
Waiting—Waiting—
Waiting?*

pattern is full size

The little chickens cuddle close,
Beneath the old hen's wings;
"Peep! Peep!" they say; "we're not afraid
of dark or anything."
So safe and sound, they nestle there,
The one beside the other,
But safe, happier, by far,
Is baby with her mother.
Mary F. Butts

Baby Animals Quilt

photo on page 8

pattern is full size

pattern is full size

pattern is full size

pattern is full size

Cute Animals Quilt

photo on page 9

pattern is full size

Peter Rabbit Apron

An apron of cream linen crash that a little girl will love to wear. It is 19 inches long, completely made. The rabbits are outlined in black floss; their suits, tinted in blue, red and yellow, are outlined with floss in contrasting colors. Peter Rabbit's tail is a black yarn pompon. Orange bias binds edges and pocket.

Pinafores, made up and tinted, with floss, 60 cents each, from Harriet Harper, Woman's World, Chicago

> *Over the silent house tops*
> *With his magic pack o'dreams,*
> *The sandman comes astealing*
> *When the golden moonlight gleams.*
> *Softly he spills the stardust,*
> *That closes our eyes in sleep,*
> *Then sets on guard his fairies*
> *Who all night vigil keep.*
>
> *Modern Priscilla September 1928*

pattern is full size

Cute Animals Quilt

photo on page 9

pattern is full size

Guardian Angels

I wonder if the twinkling stars
Are only windows bright,
Where angels watch while we're asleep,
Through all the long dark night?

J. I. Dykes

pattern is full size

Cute Animals Quilt

photo on page 9

pattern is full size

Cute Animals Quilt
photo on page 9

pattern is full size

Cute Animals Quilt

photo on page 9

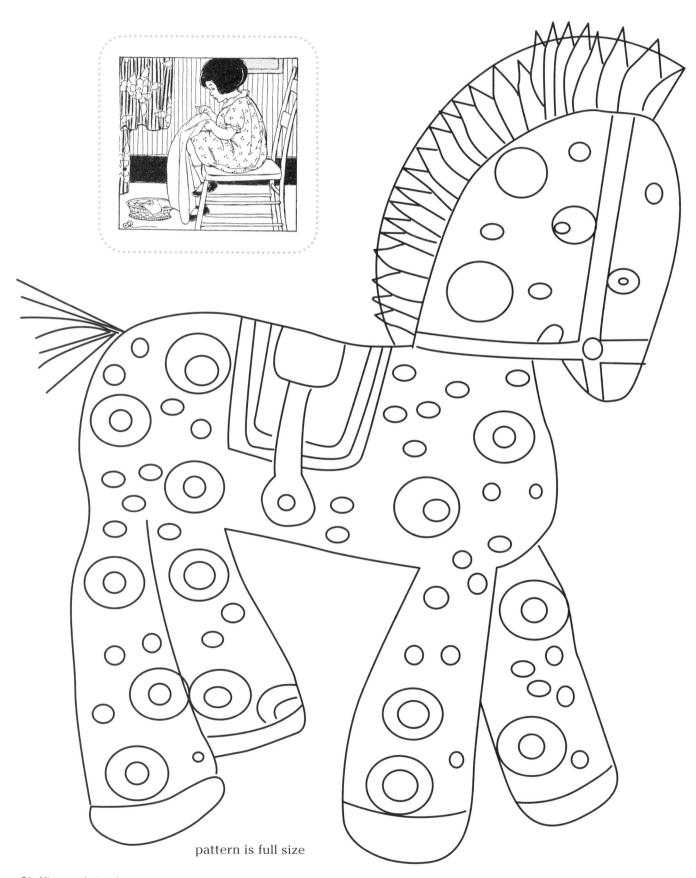

pattern is full size

pattern is full size

Cute Animals Quilt

photo on page 9

pattern is full size

pattern is full size

Cute Animals Quilt

photo on page 9

Quilt Assembly Diagram

pattern is full size

Cute Animals Quilt

FINISHED SIZE: 43" x 56½"

FABRICS:

1⅓ yard White for embroidered blocks

2¼ yards Blue for sashing, borders, backing and binding

MATERIALS:

Embroidery floss

Embroidery needle size 8

44" x 57" Batting

CUTTING:

Embroidered blocks:

12 White 12" squares

Blue horizontal sashing:

9 strips 3" x 11½"

Blue vertical sashing and borders:

4 side strips 3" x 52"

Blue top and bottom borders:

2 strips 2½" x 43½"

Binding:

Blue 2½" strips sewn together to make 200" (5 yards, 20")

INSTRUCTIONS:
1. Trace the pattern onto each White block. Embroider. Press.
   Trim blocks to 11½" x 11½".
2. See Row Assembly Diagram to sew 3 vertical rows with sashing. Press.
3. See the Quilt Assembly Diagram. Sew rows together with side border strips
and vertical sashings. Press.
4. Sew the top and bottom borders to the quilt. Press.
5. Layer backing, batting and top to form a sandwich.
   Baste the layers together. Quilt as desired.
   Trim the backing and batting to the edge of the quilt top.
6. Sew binding strips into one 200" long piece.
   Press binding in half lengthwise.
   Sew binding to the quilt front.
   Turn to the back and sew in place.

pattern is full size

Rows
Assembly Diagram

Bears Quilt

photo on page 10

pattern is full size

"Teddy Bear" Apron

No. C358 Kiddies Apron ready-made of unbleached cotton and bound in colors. Sizes 2 - 4 - 6 years, **40 cents.** Floss, 8 cents.

Just a note to all you stitchers out there - don't give up!

pattern is full size

Bears Quilt
photo on page 10

pattern is full size

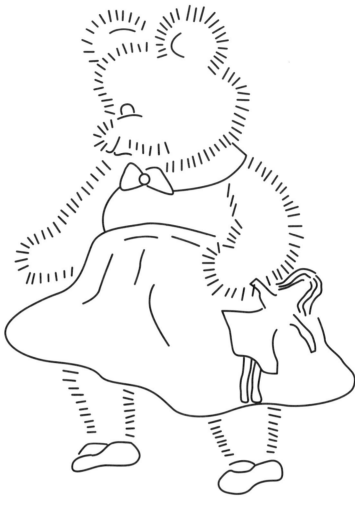

pattern is full size

Bears Quilt
photo on page 10

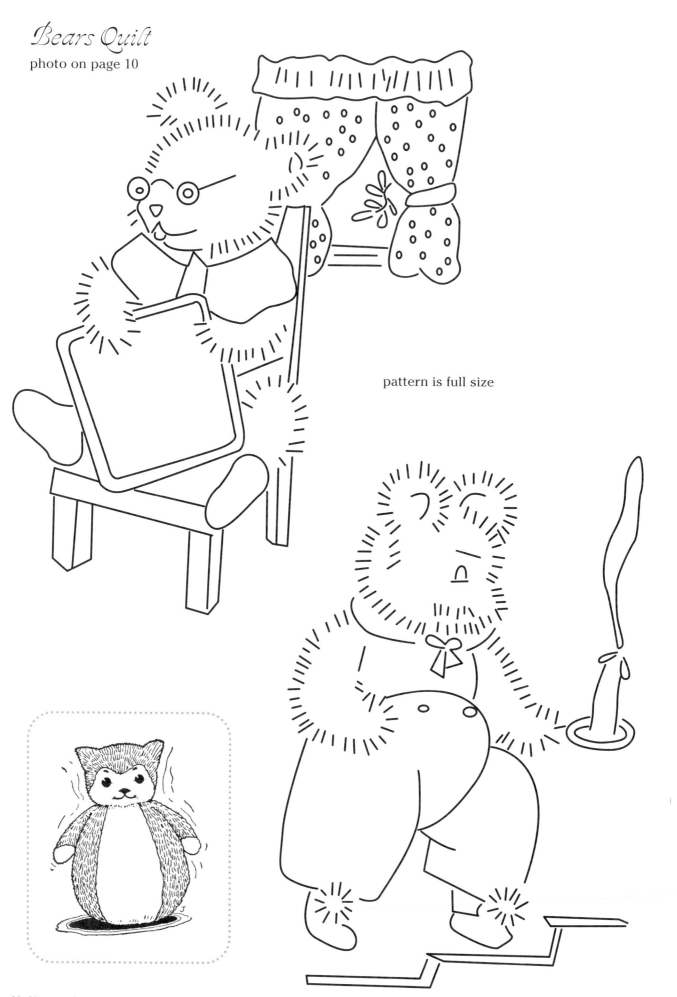

pattern is full size

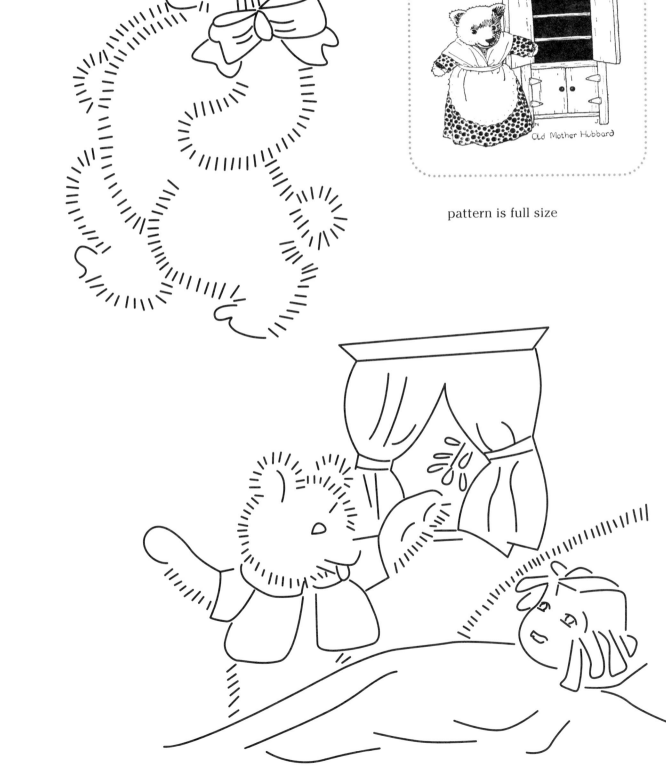

Old Mother Hubbard

pattern is full size

Bears Quilt

photo on page 10

A Prayer for Animals
Bless the animals,
Let nothing harm them;
May thy care keep them,
God, Shelter and warm them.
Lord, let them find
That people are kind!

Row Assembly Diagram

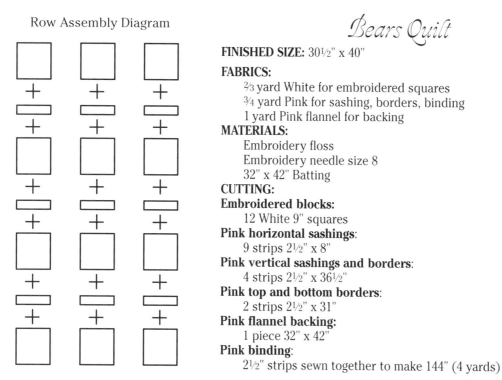

Bears Quilt

FINISHED SIZE: 30½" x 40"

FABRICS:
⅔ yard White for embroidered squares
¾ yard Pink for sashing, borders, binding
1 yard Pink flannel for backing

MATERIALS:
Embroidery floss
Embroidery needle size 8
32" x 42" Batting

CUTTING:

Embroidered blocks:
12 White 9" squares

Pink horizontal sashings:
9 strips 2½" x 8"

Pink vertical sashings and borders:
4 strips 2½" x 36½"

Pink top and bottom borders:
2 strips 2½" x 31"

Pink flannel backing:
1 piece 32" x 42"

Pink binding:
2½" strips sewn together to make 144" (4 yards)

INSTRUCTIONS:

1. Trace the pattern onto each White block. Embroider. Press.
Trim square to 8" x 8".

2. See Row Assembly Diagram. Sew 3 vertical rows with horizontal sashing strips between the blocks. Press.

3. See Quilt Assembly Diagram. Sew the rows together with vertical sashings and side borders. Sew top and bottom borders to the quilt. Press.

4. Layer backing, batting and top to form a sandwich.
Baste the layers together. Quilt as desired.
Trim the backing and batting to the edge of the quilt top.

5. Sew binding strips into one 144" long piece.
Press binding in half lengthwise.
Sew binding to the quilt front.
Turn to the back and sew in place.

Quilt Assembly Diagram

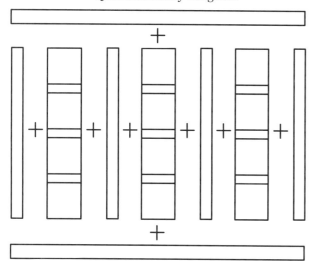

pattern is full size

pattern is full size

Numbers Summer Topper

FINISHED SIZE: 33" x 57"

FABRICS:
    1¾ yards White fabric

MATERIALS:
    Embroidery floss
    Embroidery needle
    1¾" White pom pom for tail

CUTTING:
    1 White 34½" x 58½" rectangle

INSTRUCTIONS:

1. Fold under a ⅜" hem twice all the way around the quilt. Press.
2. Blanket stitch the hem in place with Blue floss.
3. Whipstitch over the Blanket stitches with Red floss.
4. Trace the patterns onto topper.
5. Crayon tint as desired. See page 18 for Crayon Tinting instructions.
6. Embroider. Press.
7. Add pom pom tail and other embellishments as desired.

pattern is full size

pattern is full size

pattern is full size

Busy Kitties Quilt

photo on page 11

pattern is full size

pattern is full size

The Polite Kittens

My kittens have the softest fur,
And such a low, well mannered purr!

Quiet as shadows in the air,
They walk on tiptoe everywhere.

They wash their faces every day,
And clean their mittens after play.

At sleepytime they're always good,
And take a catnap as they should.

Curled up into the neatest ball,
Furry and fuzzy, round and small.

Sometimes I wish that I could be
A kitten - and so mannerly.

pattern is full size

Busy Kitties Quilt

photo on page 11

Busy Kitties Quilt

FINISHED SIZE: 37½" x 52½"

FABRICS:
  ¾ yard White for embroidered squares
  3 yards Blue for blocks, borders, backing, binding

MATERIALS:
  Embroidery floss
  Embroidery needle
  39" x 54" Batting

CUTTING:

Embroidered blocks:
  12 White 8" squares

Alternate blocks:
  12 Blue 9" squares

Border strips:
  Top/bottom strips 4¼" x 30½"
  2 side strips 4¼" x 53"

Blue backing:
  1 piece 39" x 54"

Binding:
  Blue 2½" strips sewn together to make 182"
  (5 yards, 2")

INSTRUCTIONS:

1. Trace the pattern onto each White block. Embroider. Press.
  Trim blocks to 8" x 8".

2. See Row Assembly Diagram. Sew rows together, alternating the embroidered and Blue squares. Press.

3. Sew the rows together. See Quilt Assembly Diagram. Press.

4. Add top and bottom borders. Press.

5. Sew the side borders to the quilt. Press.

6. Layer backing, batting and top to form a sandwich.
  Baste the layers together. Quilt as desired.
  Trim the backing and batting to the edge of the quilt top.

7. Sew binding strips into one 182" long piece.
  Press binding in half lengthwise.
  Sew binding to the quilt front.
  Turn to the back and sew in place.

pattern is full size

Quilt Assembly

Row Assembly Diagram

K	+	B	+	K	+	B
B	+	K	+	B	+	K
K	+	B	+	K	+	B
B	+	K	+	B	+	K
K	+	B	+	K	+	B
B	+	K	+	B	+	K

K = Kitten Block
B = Blue Fabric Block

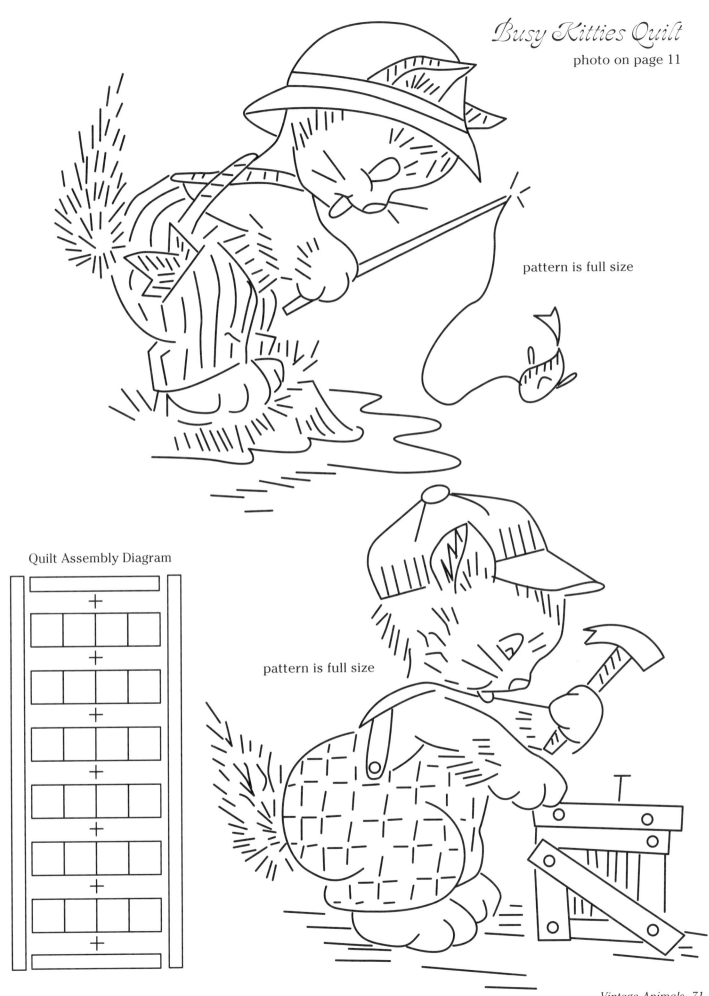

pattern is full size

Quilt Assembly Diagram

pattern is full size

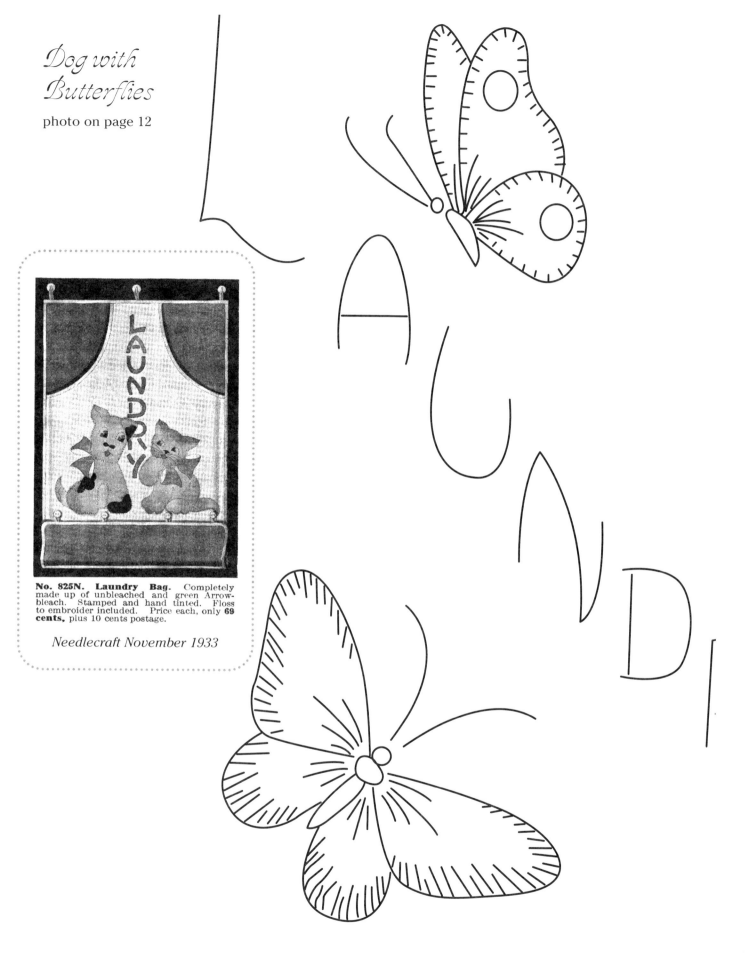

Dog with Butterflies

photo on page 12

No. 825N. **Laundry Bag.** Completely made up of unbleached and green Arrow-bleach. Stamped and hand tinted. Floss to embroider included. Price each, only **69 cents,** plus 10 cents postage.

Needlecraft November 1933

pattern is full size

Dog with Butterflies

FINISHED SIZE: 16" x 23"

FABRICS:
    1 yard White
    ⅔ yard Print

MATERIALS:
    Embroidery floss
    Embroidery needle
    4 yards bias tape
    Crayons

CUTTING:
    Cut 2 White rectangles 16" x 23".
Round the edges.
    Cut 1 Print rectangles 8½" x 16".
Round the edges.

INSTRUCTIONS:
1. Cut a 9½" slit in the front of bag following the diagram.
2. Finish slit edges with bias tape.
3. Curve the Print rectangle on the bottom to match the bag. Curve the top as shown in photo.
4. Finish the top edge of the pocket with bias tape.
5. Fold the pocket in the middle. Press. Line up the pocket with the bottom of the bag. Sew the pocket to the bag along the fold, creating 2 sections of pocket.
6. Trace the embroidery pattern onto the front of the bag.
7. Color tint as desired. See Crayon Tinting instructions on page 18.
8. Embroider design.
9. Layer front and back of bag so the edges line up.
10. Finish edges with bias tape.

Cat and Dog

photo on page 12

Cats and dogs, dogs and cats,
I've always heard they like their spats.
They're supposed to like to bark and hiss,
I can only tell you this.
The pups and pussies that I see
appear like perfect friends to me!

enlarge pattern to 160%

That little bird, he chirped to me
"Send a tune up to this tree!"
I'll grab my fiddle, grab my bow,
and make a song before I go.

connect flowers
to the lower
right corner
design

Two Pups and a Basket

photo on page 13

FINISHED SIZE: 18" x 28"

FABRICS:
   1 yard White

MATERIALS:
   Embroidery floss
   Embroidery needle
   4 yards bias tape
   Crayons

CUTTING:
   Cut 2 White rectangles 18" x 28". Round the edges.

INSTRUCTIONS:
1. Cut a 12" slit in the front of bag following the diagram.
2. Finish slit edges with bias tape.
3. Trace the embroidery pattern onto the front of the bag.
4. Color tint as desired. See Crayon Tinting instructions on page 18.
5. Embroider design.
6. Layer front and back of bag so the edges line up.
7. Finish edges with bias tape.

enlarge pattern to 160%

Embroidery Stitches

Working with Floss. Separate embroidery floss.

Use 24" lengths of floss and a #8 embroidery needle.

Use 2 to 3 ply floss to outline large elements of the design and to embroider larger and more stylized patterns.

Use 2 ply for the small details on some items.

Pay attention to backgrounds.

When working with lighter-colored fabrics, do not carry dark flosses across large unworked background areas. Stop and start again to prevent unsightly 'ghost strings' from showing through the front.

Another option is to back tinted muslin with another layer of muslin before you add embroidery stitches. This will help keep 'ghost strings' from showing.

Blanket Stitch

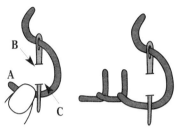

Come up at A, hold the thread down with your thumb, go down at B. Come back up at C with the needle tip over the thread. Pull the stitch into place. Repeat, outlining with the bottom legs of the stitch. Use this stitch to edge fabrics.

Chain Stitch

Come up at A. To form a loop, hold the thread down with your thumb, go down at B (as close as possible to A). Come back up at C with the needle tip over the thread. Repeat to form a chain.

Cross Stitch

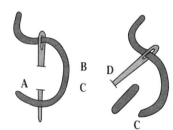

Make a diagonal Straight stitch (up at A, down at B) from upper right to lower left. Come up at C and go down at D to make another diagonal Straight stitch the same length as the first one. The stitch will form an X.

French Knot

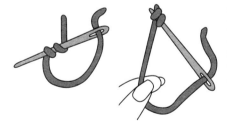

Come up at A. Wrap the floss around the needle 2 to 3 times. Insert the needle close to A. Hold the floss and pull the needle through the loops gently.

Herringbone Stitch

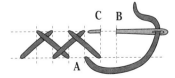 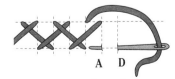

Come up at A. Make a slanted stitch to the top right, inserting the needle at B. Come up a short distance away at C.

Insert the needle at D to complete the stitch. Bring the needle back up at the next A to begin a new stitch. Repeat.

Lazy Daisy Stitch

Come up at A. Go down at B (right next to A) to form a loop. Come back up at C with the needle tip over the thread. Go down at D to make a small anchor stitch over the top of the loop.

Running Stitch

Come up at A. Weave the needle through the fabric, making short, even stitches. Use this stitch to gather fabrics, too.

Satin Stitch

Work small straight stitches close together and at the same angle to fill an area with stitches. Vary the length of the stitches as required to keep the outline of the area smooth.

Stem Stitch

Work from left to right to make regular, slanting stitches along the stitch line. Bring the needle up above the center of the last stitch. Also called 'Outline' stitch.

Straight Stitch

Come up at A and go down at B to form a simple flat stitch. Use this stitch for hair for animals and for simple petals on small flowers.

Whip Stitch

Insert the needle under a few fibers of one layer of fabric. Bring the needle up through the other layer of fabric. Use this stitch to attach the folded raw edges of fabric to the back of pieces or to attach bindings around the edges of quilts and coverlets.

Kitty Hanging Bag

photo on page 13

Kitty Hanging Bag

FINISHED SIZE: 13" x 15"

FABRICS:
⅔ yard Print for bag
6" square Pink for face

MATERIALS:
Poly-fil stuffing
Black fabric marker
1 yard Pink bias tape

CUTTING:
Cut out all pieces using pattern.

INSTRUCTIONS:

1. Cut 18" of bias tape. Fold and sew in half lengthwise. Cut into three 6" lengths.
2. Draw the face with a permanent fabric marker.
3. Head: Fold a 6" bias piece in half. Place head pieces right sides together enclosing the bias loop ends between the ears. Sew around the head leaving the neck open for stuffing. Stuff. Sew the neck closed.
4. Bag: Cut a 6" slit in the front of bag following the pattern. Finish slit edges with bias tape.
5. With right sides together, sew bag leaving the top open. Turn right side out.
6. Fold and sew and hem around the top.
7. Place cat head into the top of the bag. Gather bag to fit neck. Sew in place.
8. Sew remaining 6" strings under the neck and tie in a bow.

Binding Instructions

1. Cut the binding strips along the grain of the fabric according to the quilt instructions.
2. Sew enough strips together, end-to-end, to go around the quilt. Press seams open.
3. Fold the strip in half lengthwise, with wrong sides facing.
4. Pin the raw edge of the binding strip to align with the raw edges of the quilt top/batting/backing sandwich.
5. Machine sew the binding strip in place, stitching through all layers.
6. At the corner, leave the needle in place through the fabrics and fold the binding up straight. Fold it up and over into a mitered corner.
7. Fold the folded edge of the binding to the back and whip stitch the edge in place. Miter the corners on the front and on the back. Stitch corners closed.

Fold strip in half, wrong sides facing.

Align all raw edges.

Leave the needle in position at the corner. Fold the binding up and back to miter.

pattern is full size

Helpful Hint

To make sharp, clean corners, come up at A, go down at B. Come up at C (at corner) with needle tip over thread. Go down at D to secure loop at corner, come back up at B.

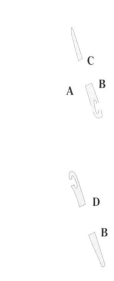

cat dress pattern is full size
Place on Fold and cut 2
Slit front of dress from top 6"

Light Cat Face

photo on page 13

pattern is full size

Red Cat Face

photo on page 13

This dog of mine is dear, I think,
His nose is cool, his tongue is pink,
His heart is warm, his eye is bright;
I love him, oh, with all my might.

For when I'm happy, he and I,
Go skipping off beneath the sky;
We rove the fields and range afar,
Where birds and trees and flowers are.

Julius King

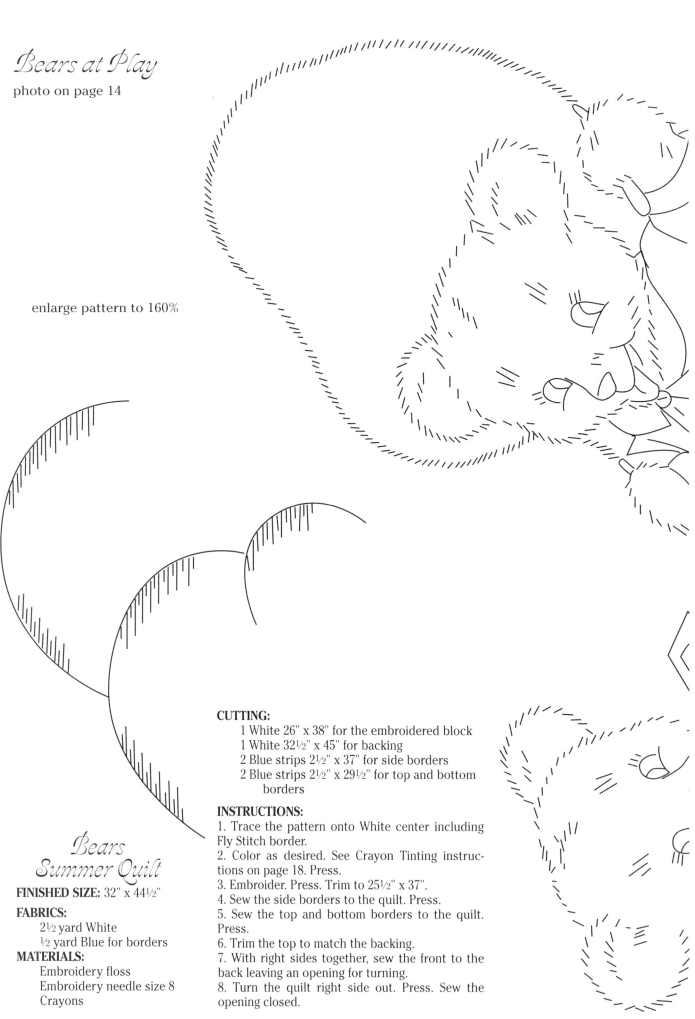

Bears at Play

photo on page 14

enlarge pattern to 160%

CUTTING:
1 White 26" x 38" for the embroidered block
1 White 32½" x 45" for backing
2 Blue strips 2½" x 37" for side borders
2 Blue strips 2½" x 29½" for top and bottom
borders

INSTRUCTIONS:
1. Trace the pattern onto White center including Fly Stitch border.
2. Color as desired. See Crayon Tinting instructions on page 18. Press.
3. Embroider. Press. Trim to 25½" x 37".
4. Sew the side borders to the quilt. Press.
5. Sew the top and bottom borders to the quilt. Press.
6. Trim the top to match the backing.
7. With right sides together, sew the front to the back leaving an opening for turning.
8. Turn the quilt right side out. Press. Sew the opening closed.

Bears Summer Quilt

FINISHED SIZE: 32" x 44½"

FABRICS:
2½ yard White
½ yard Blue for borders

MATERIALS:
Embroidery floss
Embroidery needle size 8
Crayons

enlarge pattern to 160%

Three Little Pigs

photo on page 14

Three Little Pigs Summer Quilt

FINISHED SIZE: 31½" x 42½"

FABRICS:
  2½ yards White
  ⅓ yard Blue

MATERIALS:
  Embroidery floss
  Embroidery needle
  Crayons

CUTTING:
  1 White 27½" x 38½" for embroidered center
  1 White 33" x 44" for backing
  2 Blue strips 2¾" x 27½" for top and bottom borders
  2 Blue strips 2¾" x 42½" for side borders

INSTRUCTIONS:
1. Trace the pattern onto White center.
2. Color tint as desired. See Crayon Tinting instructions on page 18. Press.
3. Sew the top and bottom border strips to the topper. Press.
4. Sew the side borders to the topper. Press.
5. Trim the top to match the backing.
6. With right sides together, sew the front to the back leaving an opening for turning.
7. Turn the quilt right side out. Press. Sew the opening closed.
8. Topstitch around edges if desired.

enlarge pattern to 160%

Three Little Pigs

photo on page 14

enlarge pattern to 160%

Bunnies on a Bicycle

photo on page 15

Bunnies Summer Quilt

FINISHED SIZE: 34" x 45"

FABRICS:
   2½ yards White

MATERIALS:
   Embroidery floss
   Embroidery needle
   Crayons
   4 yards each Blue and Pink rickrack

CUTTING:
   2 White 34½" x 45½"

INSTRUCTIONS:
1. Trace the pattern onto White center.
2. Color tint as desired. See Crayon Tinting instructions on page 18. Press.
3. Embroider. Press.
4. Position the Blue rickrack 3" from the edge. Sew in place.
5. Position the Pink rickrack 4" from the edge. Sew in place.
6. With right sides together, sew the front to the back leaving an opening for turning.
7. Turn quilt right side out. Press. Sew opening closed.

enlarge pattern to 160%

enlarge pattern to 160%

Seesaw

photo on page 15

border pattern

enlarge pattern to 160%

Seesaw Summer Quilt

FINISHED SIZE: 34" x 44"

FABRICS:
1⅓ yards White cotton fabric
1⅓ yards White flannel fabric

MATERIALS:
Embroidery floss
Embroidery needle
5 yards White satin blanket binding

CUTTING:
1 White cotton 35" x 45" rectangle
1 White flannel 34" x 44" rectangle

INSTRUCTIONS:
1. Draw border pattern 4" from the top and bottom, 2½" from the sides.
2. Trace the embroidery patterns.
3. Crayon tint as desired. See page 18 for Crayon Tinting instructions.
4. Embroider. Press. Trim to match the White flannel back.
5. Layer the top and back without batting. Quilt as desired.
6. Finish edges with blanket binding.

enlarge pattern to 160%

Puppy Pot holders

photo on page 15

enlarge pattern
to 120%

enlarge pattern
to 120%

POTS=PANS

enlarge pattern to
160%

enlarge pattern to 160%

enlarge pattern to 160%

Priscilla at her Sampler
Sets stitches neat and fine,
But sweet Prunella's stitches
Won't last as long as mine.

For Prunella never guesses —
And I haven't told her yet —
That in my heart she's stitching
Her own dear silhouette!

Constance Vivien Frazier
Needlecraft September 1926

Needlecraft Helps

By MRS. L. C. HEATH

No need for our hands to be folded,
There are always such beautiful things;
And ever we're anxiously waiting
The pleasures that Needlecraft brings.
We find every page so inviting,
Something new for our eyes to behold;
We may fill our desires by just writing—
How to do things so clearly is told.

With hooks and with shuttles and needles,
We study the pages all o'er,
And fill up our boxes with samples
From Needlecraft's wonderful store.
Every piece has its tested directions,
So easily followed, we find,
As we're counting the dear little stitches
While working each different kind.

Let us draw up our chairs in a circle,
Much nearer than ever before,
And our praises of Needlecraft echo
For its pages of patterns galore.
Let us vow we will give it a welcome,
And never will turn it away;
Let it dwell in our homes as a token
Of everything useful and gay!

Needlecraft March 1925

enlarge pattern to 160%

pattern is full size

enlarge pattern to 160%

enlarge pattern
to 120%

enlarge pattern to 160%

Cat and Dog
photo on page 99

See Embroidery Stitches on page 77

No. 826N. Pillow. Stamped on orange rayon. Felt patches and floss to embroider included. Price each, only **69 cents,** plus 10 cents postage. Send your orders to
NEEDLECRAFT MAGAZINE
Augusta, Maine

Needlecraft November 1933

enlarge pattern to 160%

Popular Pillows

There is no end to the variety of pillow designs over the decades. Stitching has been an undying favorite for use with this necessary and decorative accessory.

Tinted and stitched combos are a great way to lend a touch of the days gone by to any room, especially the nursery. They are also a great project for someone learning or in a hurry.

Tinting and embroidery go together easily and are a good "starter" project when trying a new technique like tinting.

Three Bears and Two Geese

Yellow is a good pick when stitching a pillow for an expectant mother - you can hedge your bets.

patterns on pages 96 - 97

Cat and Dog

Is it love at first sight or just a truce from the fight?

For the moment these two seem to be getting along.

pattern on page 98

Wonderful Projects for Embroidery!

Additional Books on Creativity...

5214

5270

5290

Design Originals

www.d-originals.com

2425 CULLEN STREET
FORT WORTH, TX 76107